By Walter Hirsch
& Fred Rose

TRADITIONAL JAZZ SERIES

CHICAGO-STYLE
JAM SESSION

3921

MMO 3921

MUSIC MINUS ONE

3921

TRADITIONAL JAZZ SERIES

CHICAGO-STYLE JAM SESSION

ABOUT THIS RECORDING

THE MUSIC MINUS ONE TRADITIONAL JAZZ SERIES has been carefully conceived to address key elements of performance in early jazz styles. There are many offshoots of New Orleans jazz that make up a broad continuum of divergent styles from Ragtime to Mainstream. Such labels are important for identification only and their use is to encourage creativity through stylistic integrity.

This volume, *Chicago-Style Jam Session,* emphasizes collectively improvised ensembles and the succession of individual solos. These generally unstructured ensembles are a key element of this freewheeling style. The rhythmic texture is rooted in the swing feel of the late 1930s, and the instrumentation is typical of the New York groups of this genre. The songs are popular melodies from the 1900s to 1930s as well as multithematic compositions and blues.

Sometimes this style is referred to as the New York-Chicago style, sometimes as post-Chicago style. It has also been called "Nicksieland," a play on "Dixieland" that recognizes a Greenwich Village nightclub called "Nick's," where this music was showcased in the 1950s. Chicago-style jazz is named for the city where it first developed. In the 1920s, many New Orleans musicians, including Joe "King" Oliver, Jimmy Noone, Johnny and "Baby" Dodds, Freddie Keppard, "Jelly Roll" Morton, Louis Armstrong, the Original Dixieland Jazz Band, and the New Orleans Rhythm Kings actively performed and recorded in Chicago. There are also many younger musicians around Chicago who were profoundly influenced by their music, including Eddie Condon, Benny Goodman, Gene Krupa, Muggsy Spanier, Bud Freeman and many others. By the 1930s many of these same musicians moved on to New York. Some continued to perform in the New Orleans tradition and others became significant figures of the Swing era. As the Big Band era closed, improvising soloists still found work in New York clubs such as Nick's, Eddie Condon's and the Metropole. The texture was distinctly in the New Orleans tradition but the language was Swing and directly reflected the synthesis that took place in Chicago.

The musicians chosen for this session are, in a way, exponents of this tradition. Their personal styles are amalgamations of the greatest stylists who preceded them. You can hear in Hal Smith aural glimpses of Dave Tough and George Wettling. You can hear in Jon-Erik shades of Muggsy Spanier and Wild Bill Davison. Brian Ogilvie's voice of choice is flavored by the sonorities of Bud Freeman and Eddie Miller, and I myself owe more than a little bit to Edmond Hall's style. The other musicians were chosen for these qualities as well, and as a result, this stylistically accurate recording demonstrates the inner workings of collective improvisation in a traditional jazz context.

THE SONGS:

ROSETTA: This 1933 composition by stride pianist Earl "Fatha" Hines has long been a popular jam session standard.

'DEED I DO: From 1926, this is another well-worn standard that really swings.

BLUES (MY NAUGHTY SWEETIE GIVES TO ME): This was composed in 1919 and is not actually a blues as the title might imply. Many publishers did this to capitalize on the "blues" craze.

SUGAR: This was a 1926 hit by Maceo Pinkard and popularized by singers including Billie Holiday and Bessie Smith.

THE DARKTOWN STRUTTER'S BALL: A unique 20-bar form. This popular song, from 1917, is still very much a traditional jazz standard. The composer, Shelton Brooks, is also known for "Some of These Days" and "Walkin' the Dog".

ROYAL GARDEN BLUES: The Williams brothers had their own publishing company in Chicago and wrote this in 1919. It is a multi-theme composition with a built-in modulation. Named after a Chicago dance hall, it is an interesting treatment of the 12-bar blues form.

POOR BUTTERFLY: This classic ballad was composed in 1916. The melody and harmonies are wonderfully sophisticated and unique. Although in general we endeavored to stay true to the original, this recording has implemented a few chord changes that reflect the way the song is generally performed.

THAT'S A PLENTY: From 1914, this is a classic "warhorse" of the genre. It is a multi-theme composition with a 16-bar chorus. The full band performance reflects the typical harmony parts that are derived from the original orchestration.

HOW TO USE THIS RECORDING

Listen carefully to hear how the parts weave together. Use the melody cues and chord symbols to guide your harmonies and find the most logical places to add your voice to the texture. Remember: collective improvisation is not everyone making a solo simultaneously. The role of the instruments in the ensemble passages is to provide melodic and rhythmic counterpoint to the lead voice while emphasizing pivotal harmonic relationships. Essentially, you are spontaneously creating an orchestration. Precise ensemble figures have been avoided to provide soloists with maximum freedom and to stay true to the Chicago style. Great care has been taken to optimize the potential development of many important skills: melodic interpretation and embellishment, collective improvisation in a typical "front line," solo improvisation with a swing rhythm section, leadsheet reading skills, sight transposition, and using and following head arrangements. Besides instrument specific arrangements, this book includes concert leadsheets for all of the songs with a "roadmap." This is a reflection of the professional standard for performance in this idiom, since it is generally unwritten. Challenge yourself first by learning the songs and then by using the leadsheet roadmaps as if the bandleader is telling you the arrangement off the top of his/her head.

The "B" disc in this package contains a special slow-tempo version of each piece which can be used as you get yourself "up to speed," and which may help you as you experiment with your own improvisations.

Trombone

Rosetta

by Earl Hines

Trombone

'Deed I Do

by Walter Hirsch
& Fred Rose

Trombone

Blues
(My Naughty Sweetie Gives to Me)

by Swanstone,
McCarron & Morgan

MMO 3921

Trombone

Sugar
(That Sugar Baby o'Mine)

By Maceo Pinkard, Edna B. Pinkard
and Sidney D. Mitchell

The Darktown Strutters' Ball

by Shelton Brooks

Trombone

Royal Garden Blues

by Clarence & Spencer Williams

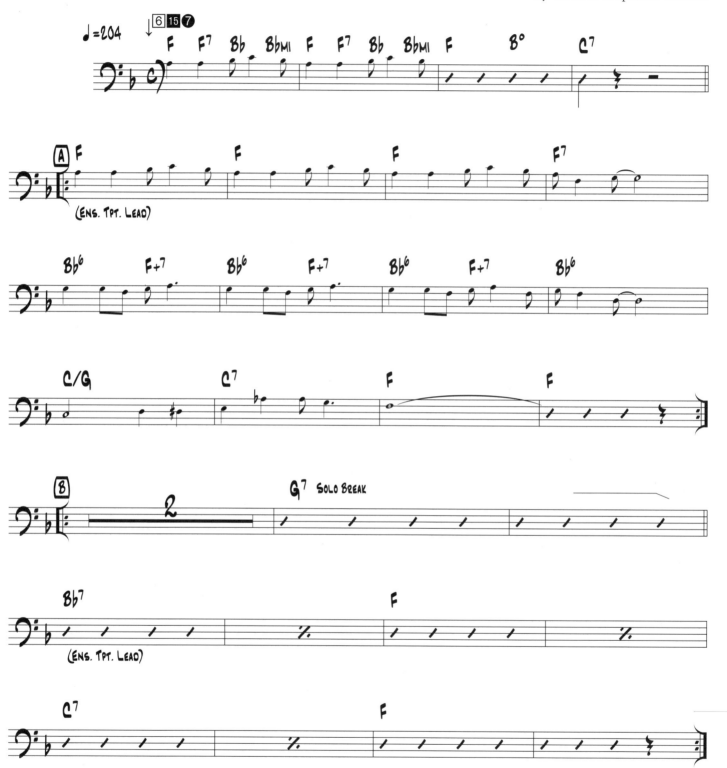

Trombone

Poor Butterfly

by John Golden
& Raymond Hubbell

MMO 3921

MMO 3921

That's A Plenty

by Ray Gilbert
& Lew Pollack

Concert Lead Sheet

Rosetta

4 Bar Piano Intro
Solo Lead
Ens. Tpt. Lead
Open Solos (3X)
Ens. Tpt. Lead
4-Bar Drum Tag, 4 Bar Ens. Tag

by Earl Hines
& William Henri Wood

Concert Lead Sheet

'Deed I Do

8 Bar Piano Intro
Solo Melody
Ensemble (Tpt. Lead)
Open Solos (3X on CD)
Ensemble Out Chorus (Tpt. Lead)
Bass Solo on Bridge

By Walter Hirsch
& Fred Rose

MMO 3921

Concert Lead Sheet

Blues
(My Naughty Sweetie Gives to Me)

Last 8 Ens. Intro
Solo Melody 8, Ens. 8, Solo 8, Ens. 8
Ensemble (Tpt Lead)
Open Solos (2x on CD)
Trade 4's (1x)
Ensemble Out Chorus (Tpt Lead)
4 Bar Drum Tag, Last 8 Ens. w/Double Ending

by Swanstone,
McCarron
& Morgan

MMO 3921

Sugar
(That Sugar Baby o'Mine)

4 Bar Piano Intro
1X Solo Lead, 1X Ens. Tpt Lead
Open Solos 1 1/2 X
Ens. Tpt. Lead From Bridge Out

by Maceo Pinkard, Edna B. Pinkard
& Sidney D. Mitchell

MMO 3921

The Darktown Strutters' Ball

Last 8 Ens. w/solo breaks
Ensemble (Tpt Lead)
Open Solos (3x)
Soft Ens.
Ensemble Out Chorus (Tpt Lead)
   Tag last 8 3x w/breaks (Bone, Clar, Tpt, Tenor, Drums)

by Shelton Brooks

Royal Garden Blues

ENS. INTRO
2X VERSE [A] 2X BREAK STRAIN [B]
4 BAR MODULATION [C]
2X CHORUS, OPEN SOLOS (8X) [D]
OUT CHORUSES (3X) [D]
4 BAR DRUM TAG, 4 BAR ENS TAG

by Clarence & Spencer Williams

MMO 3921

Poor Butterfly

Last 8 Guitar Intro
Solo Melody
Open Solo Chorus
1/2 Chorus Ens. Tpt Lead
Solo Lead (8 bars)
Ens. Tpt Lead Last 8 w/ritard

by John Golden
& Raymond Hubbell

That's A Plenty

Ens. Tpt. Lead [A] [B] [A] (Slight Variation)
Ens. Chorus [C]
Interlude (Dogfight) [D]
Open Solos [C]   (8X on CD)
Dogfight [D]
Ens. Out Choruses [C]   (3X on CD)
4 Bar Drum Tag, 4 Bar Ens. Tag

by Ray Gilbert
& Lew Pollack

MMO 3921

THE MUSICIANS

MIKE PITTSLEY (trombone)

A California native, Mike spent just over 20 years with the Jim Cullum Jazz Band. The versatility and high standard of this renowned traditional jazz band gave Mike the opportunity to really hone his craft, and the nationally syndicated radio program "Riverwalk" has showcased Mike on over 110 shows. Backing artists such as Benny Carter, Joe Williams, Dick Hyman, Lionel Hampton, and countless others are among his career highlights. In this genre, Mike considers trombonist Abram "Abe" Lincoln to be his greatest influence. To honor his mentor, Mike recorded this entire MMO session on Abe's 1930s vintage Bach trombone. This very horn can be heard on all of Abe's sessions from the 1950s with the Rampart St. Paraders as well as the Chicago-style paradigm recording "Coast Concert" with Bobby Hackett and Jack Teagarden.

EVAN CHRISTOPHER (clarinet and leader)

Permanently based in New Orleans, Evan Christopher has established himself as one of the most spirited proponents of the traditional-jazz clarinet styles. His studies, which began at age 11, earned him the Louis Armstrong Jazz Award as a teen, and after university studies in Southern California he moved to New Orleans. His activities included a broad variety of work with traditional jazz musicians including Al Hirt, Lars Edegran, and veterans of Preservation Hall. In 1996, he joined Jim Cullum's Jazz Band in San Antonio, Texas for a stint that lasted just over two years and included appearances with musical guests including Dick Hyman and William Warfield. Currently, various recording projects, a busy international touring schedule, and research on the Creole clarinet style are all endeavors that show his commitment to creative music rooted in early jazz.

JON-ERIK KELLSO (trumpet)

Raised in Detroit, Jon-Erik began his craft at age 11. His love for early jazz styles found him at 17 featured alongside Wild Bill Davidson and a member of James Dapogny's Chicago Jazz Band in the late 1980s. In 1989 he moved to New York City to join Vince Giordano's Nighthawks and was quickly welcomed into mainstream and traditional jazz circles. Credits include performances and recordings with jazz veterans including Ralph Sutton, Kenny Davern, Milt Hinton, Dick Hyman, and Doc Cheatham. Keeping the tradition alive, Two Arbors Records releases showcase his talents as a leader, and work with "nouveau swing" divas such as Peggy Cone and Ingrid Lucia have gained him recognition as one of the best swing trumpet soloists on the jazz scene.

BRIAN OGILVIE (tenor saxophone)

After a three-year stint in the mid-1990s with the renowned Jim Cullum Jazz Band of San Antonio, Texas, this Vancouver, Canada native moved to New Orleans. A hard-swinging virtuoso on saxophone and clarinet, Brian has worked and recorded with jazz legends including Joe Williams, Harry "Sweets" Edison, and Dick Hyman. Work as a featured soloist in the company of mainstream stalwarts such as Dan Barrett and Harry Allen find him touring regularly in Europe and in the U.S. "For You," an Arbors release under his own name, and countless others as a sideman, document his passion and enthusiasm for early jazz styles.

JEFF BARNHART (piano)

A versatile pianist and entertainer, Jeff is an enthusiastic performer devoted to showcasing early jazz piano styles. Ragtime, boogie, stride and swing are his specialties and he keeps them fresh and vital through work as a soloist, educator, and recording artist. Recordings on Jeff's own label, Jazz Alive Records, represent a sizable catalog of his work, and concert appearances as a soloist as well as with swing and traditional-jazz festival bands find him enjoying a busy touring schedule in both the U.S. and the U.K. Jeff got hooked on the traditional jazz sound early when he heard Eddie Condon's recording, "That Toddlin' Town" and cites Jess Stacey and Earl Hines as two very strong influences for this style.

BILL HUNTINGTON (guitar)

Born in New Orleans in 1937, Bill Huntington is in many ways the quintessential New Orleans artist. Bill's first instrument at the age of 12 was banjo, which he studied with Lawrence Marrero. He switched to guitar at 16 and later to string bass. His deep roots in early jazz have kept him in great demand. Credits include recordings with many traditional jazz legends, among them Percy Humphrey, Pete Fountain, Al Hirt, Raymond Burke, Doc Cheatham and Bucky Pizzarelli. Bill can be heard regularly with Ellis Marsalis and is also active in jazz education both locally at the University of New Orleans and as a clinician in the U.S. and abroad.

JIM SINGLETON (bass)

Bassist James Singleton, one of the busiest in New Orleans, is a conduit of pure energy whose solid rhythmic concept and intuitive stylistic adaptability is the foundation of any group in which he performs. He has appeared with swing and traditional greats Clarence "Gatemouth" Brown, Lionel Hampton, and Arnette Cobb as well as many modern jazz musicians such as John Abercrombie, John Scofield, Art Baron, Ellis Marsalis, and Eddie Harris. His extensive recording credits include work with Chet Baker, Alvin "Red" Tyler, and James Booker and his own groups "3 Now 4" and "Astral Project."

HAL SMITH (drums)

Hal's passion for the early styles of jazz, of course, is evident in his swinging performances and recordings, but also in his tireless efforts as a journalist for publications such as the Mississippi Rag, as a producer of recordings by artists including Lu Watters and Ben Pollack, and as an educator for traditional jazz projects such as the AFCDJS Traditional Jazz Camp. Based near San Diego, California, Hal has established himself as an integral part of the West-Coast traditional jazz scene but frequently travels for work as a soloist, recording artist, and bandleader. Associations include appearances and recordings with Bob Wilber, Kenny Davern, Ed Polcer, Wild Bill Davison, Ralph Sutton, and Doc Cheatham. His drumming style is an encyclopedic amalgam of his favorites, among them "Baby" Dodds, George Wettling, Paul Barbarin, Gene Krupa, Sid Catlett, Nick Fatool, Zutty Singleton, Dave Tough and Ben Pollack.

Photos: Irv Kratka

MMO 3921

MUSIC MINUS ONE
50 Executive Boulevard
Elmsford, New York 10523-1325
800-669-7464 (U.S.)/914-592-1188 (International)

www.musicminusone.com
e-mail: mmogroup@musicminusone.com

Printed in Canada